Notes to Beethoven's Concerto in B flat

By FRANZ KULLAK

This Second Concerto, according to the composer's own statement*, was composed earlier than the one published as op. 15, in C major. Although Beethoven himself did not style his work "The Second," but simply "Concert" (or "Concerto"), he nevertheless gave rise, by appending the opus-number "19," to the current designation.

The apparent reason for this was, that when he entered into negotiations with Hoffmeister, his publisher, he had no lower opus-number at his disposal**. But the Concerto was finished before the publication of the three trios, op. 1 (Oct., 1795). The period of its composition is set by Nottebohm between the first half of 1794 and Mar. 29, 1795, which he designates as the probable date of the first performance***.

The autograph of the score, which, according to Nottebohm (Them. Catalogue, 2nd ed.), was in private hands as late as 1868, is at present in the possession of the Royal Library at Berlin. For the first two movements, there are only a few fragments of the pianoforte-part, some of them being different readings; for the third, somewhat further developed passages, but also fragmentary (sketches), some indicated only in one hand.

The reading of the solo piano-part, in the present edition, follows in general an edition of Hoffmeister & Co. (No. 65, oblong)†.

Orchestral parts, evidently from the same publishing-house, and likewise marked "65," we have designated, briefly, as "Original Parts." Our reading of the orchestral portion has been carefully compared with the Autograph.

We have indicated staccato by dots only. (Dots appear originally only in measures 2 and 6 of the second solo.) In the case of the turn-sign ∾, we follow the (more rational) modern usage of placing a chromatic sign altering the *lower* auxiliary, *below* the turn-sign. We did not metrically divide the ♪♪♪♪♪♪, as Beethoven (at least in the Concertos) evidently makes no distinction between ♪♪♪♪♪ and ♪♪♪♪♪♪. (*Cf.* the *Largo* of the C-minor Concerto.) Emendations of the text of other editions, mentioned in the Notes, are supported *inter alia* by the following sources: For the score-parts, by the *orchestral parts* copied (and probably revised by the composer himself) from the Autograph; for the solo pianoforte-part, by the *Autograph* (or the copy) of the pianoforte-part.

---

* In a letter to Breitkopf & Härtel. The fact was established by Nottebohm, by comparing Beethoven's musical sketches ("Mus. Wochenblatt," VI, No. 48).

** Letter of Dec. 15, 1800, to Hoffmeister. [Thayer, II, 109.] According to Nottebohm's Thematic Catalogue, Second Edition, op. 15, 16 and 17 appeared in March, 1801; op. 18, Part I, in the summer, and Part II in October of that year (publ. by Mollo & Co., Vienna); and op. 19 towards the end of 1801.

*** "Mus. Wochenblatt" No. 48 (Nov. 26, 1875).—Thayer (I, p. 249) assumes that the Concerto played on the above date was already the C-major Concerto. For details, see the passage noted.

† The full title of this edition is as follows:
"Concert / pour le / Pianoforte / avec deux Violons, Viole, Violoncelle et Basse, / une Flûte, 2 Oboes, 2 Cors, 2 Bassons, / composé et dédié / à Monsieur Charles Nikl / Noble de Nikelsberg, Conseiller aulique / de sa¹ Majesté Impériale et Royale / par / Louis van Beethoven. / Œuvre XIX. / à Vienne chez Hoffmeister² & Comp. : / à Leipsic au Bureau de Musique. / No. 65³. Prix⁴ 2 Rthlr. 12 ggr.:—This was, according to Thayer ("Chronological Catalogue," No. 58), the original edition.—Nottebohm says (Th., V, Second Edition): "Title of the earliest edition, published towards the end of 1801 by Hoffmeister & Kühnel (Bureau de Musique) at Leipzig: 'Concerto, etc.'"—"Concerto." is given on p. 2 of the edition aforesaid.
¹Thayer gives "Sa." ²Another proof from the original plates has in place of the words "à Vienne chez Hoffmeister & Comp." the words "chez A. Kühnel." (Between 1806 and 1814.) ³Omitted by Thayer. ⁴Omitted by Thayer and Nottebohm.

Second Concerto.

Dedicated to C. Nikl, Edler von Nikelsberg.

Published, in this arrangement, 1881.
Revised, 1885.

L. van BEETHOVEN, Op. 19.

Allegro con brio. (M.M. ♩ = 132; acc. to Czerny,(1) ♩ = 152.)

(1) Carl Czerny: "Die Kunst des Vortrags der ältern und neuern Claviercompositionen" [The Art of Interpreting Early and Modern Compositions for the Pianoforte], Supplement to the Great Pianoforte-Method. op. 500.— Is not the "5" in "152" an engraver's mistake?

(2) Flute, 2 Oboes, 2 Bassoons, 2 Horns in Bb, and String-quartet (quintet).— In arranging the orchestral part of this Concerto, the editor thought it best to place ease of execution above completeness of harmony.

(3) Here we follow, with regard to the bass, the reading of the original bass part which has also been adopted in the printed scores (Breitkopf & Härtel; Peters).— In the Autograph, this is changed, by a later correction, to

SCHIRMER'S LIBRARY
OF MUSICAL CLASSICS

Vol. 622

LUDWIG VAN BEETHOVEN

Op. 19

Concerto No. II

For the Piano

Provided with Fingering, and with a
Complete Arrangement, for Piano,
of the Orchestral Accompaniment

by

FRANZ KULLAK

The Introduction and Notes
translated from the German
by
DR. THEODORE BAKER

ISBN 0-7935-5705-4

G. SCHIRMER, Inc.

DISTRIBUTED BY

 HAL•LEONARD®
CORPORATION

7777 W. BLUEMOUND RD. P.O. BOX 13819 MILWAUKEE, WI 53213

(1) The *sf* belongs, according to the Autograph, to this syncopation, not to the preceding one.

(1)
Originally:

(The bass-notes in the Tutti, as usual, with large heads; expression-marks of same size both for Tutti and Solo.)

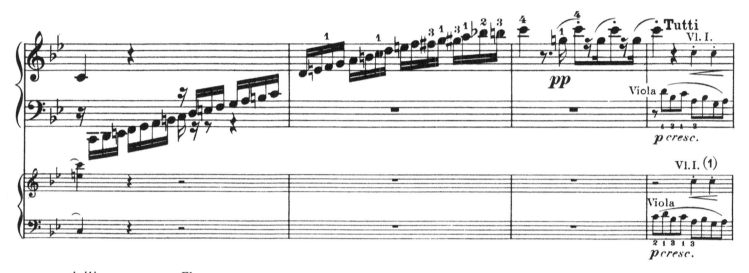

(1) Slur and $\diagdown$ are wanting in the Autograph here and in the parallel passage on p. 19. (Were they cross-ed out the first time? Quite illegible.) The slur is also omitted in both passages in the original violin - part; Hoffmeister's pianoforte - part gives, in this place, ; in the parallel passage, no sign whatever. (Bassoon I has, in the original part, only staccato-dots without a slur; in the Autograph, no sign at all.)

(1) Originally: 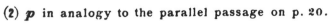 etc. Trill with lower appoggiatura. Played: etc.

(2) *p* in analogy to the parallel passage on p. 20.

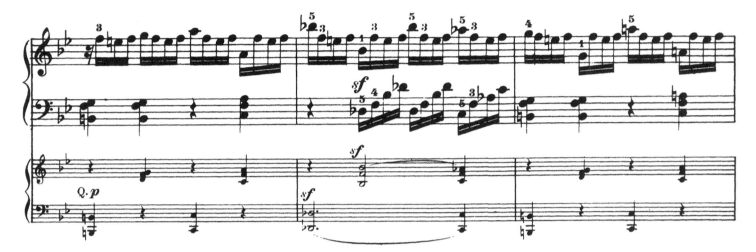

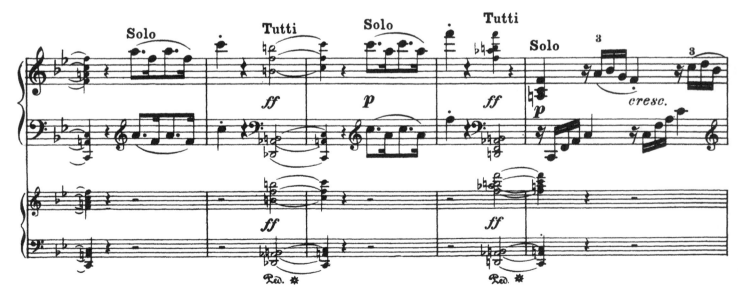

(1) In the bass (by mistake?) originally

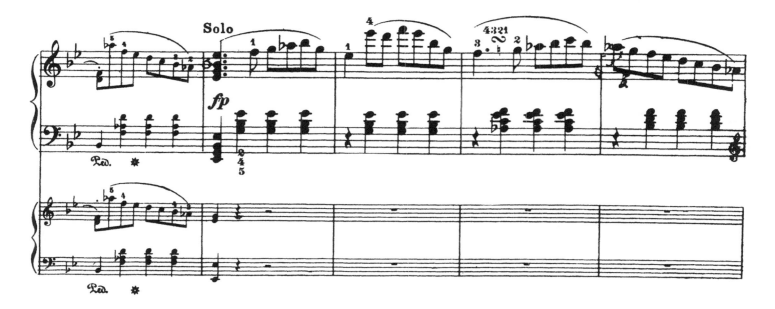

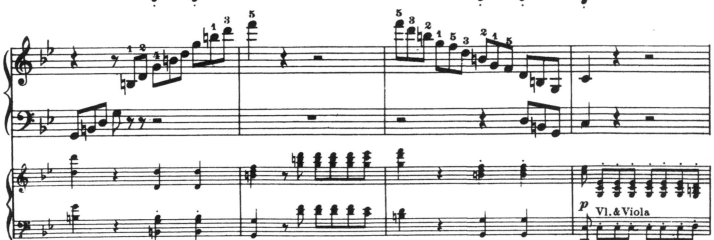

(1) "Senza sordino", *with pedal;* "con sordino", *without pedal* (✳). — It is best, with our modern pianos, to take the pedal anew with each measure, and to release it during the scale.

(2)

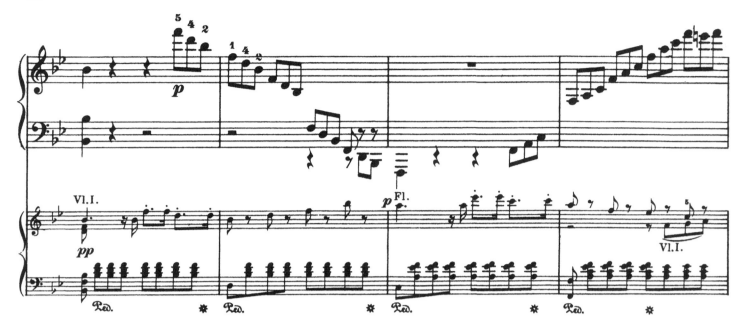

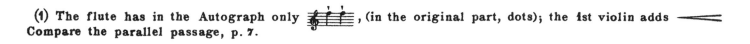

(1) The flute has in the Autograph only ♪ , (in the original part, dots); the 1st violin adds ⟋⟍
Compare the parallel passage, p. 7.

(1) Did the composer forget the *sf*? — Compare the parallel passage, p. 10.

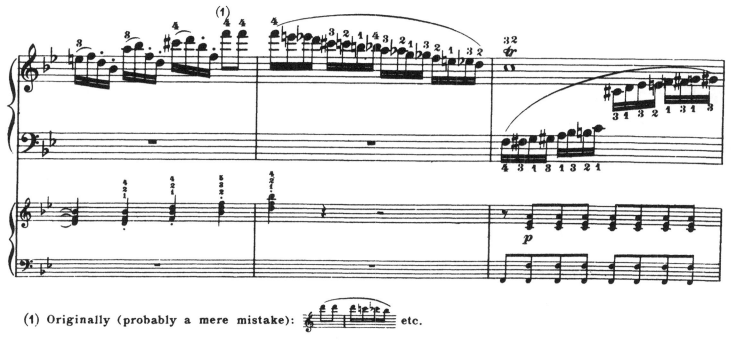

(1) Originally (probably a mere mistake): ♯ 𝅘𝅥𝅘𝅥 𝅘𝅥𝅘𝅥 etc.

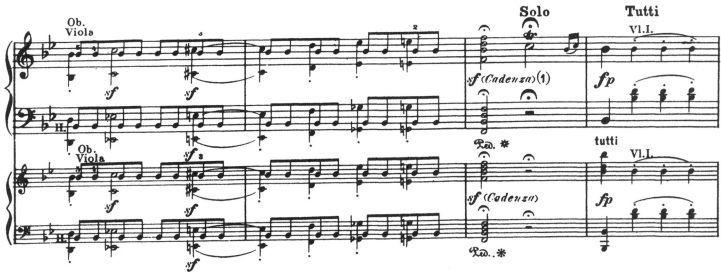

(1) For Cadenza by Beethoven, see Appendix.

Adagio. (M.M. ♩ = 80; acc. to Czerny, = 84.)

(1) This *f* is inadvertently omitted in the original Tutti-arrangement (but not the preceding *ff*). — Breitkopf & Härtel add *f* at beginning of Solo; Peters adds only the *f* in the Tutti.

(1) Corrected, in Peters and Breitkopf & Härtel, thus:  or thus:

(2) Originally: etc. (in large note-heads). The notation of the figure in the second measure is inexact, compared with the Autograph and the original parts.

(3) Dotted bars added by the editor, to facilitate reading.

(1) According to the original parts, and the Autograph, *cresc.* (not *cresc. poco*).

(2) Was a "*cresc.*" forgotten here? Compare the following *decresc.*, which to be sure, passes over into *pp.* — The *cresc.* missed by us occurs (though not till the beginning of the following measure) in later editions of the *Bureau de Musique de C. F. Peters.* One of these editions is entitled: *Deuxième Concert....Nouvelle Edition, revue et corrigée.**) *Leipzig,* etc...*Pr. 2½ Thlr. (Pour Piano seul 1 Thlr.)* "[Register: 65.] — The title of the other reads: *Deuxième Grand Concert...arrangé avec deux Violins, Viola et Violoncelle et augmenté d'une Cadence par Charles Czerny... Pr. 2 Thlr.*" [Register: 3695.]

*) "*par l'auteur*" is doubtless *not* appended. — The largely increased number of expression-marks in the last movement, greatly resembling those in the following edition (Czerny's), admit of the possibility that Czerny also had a hand in this edition.

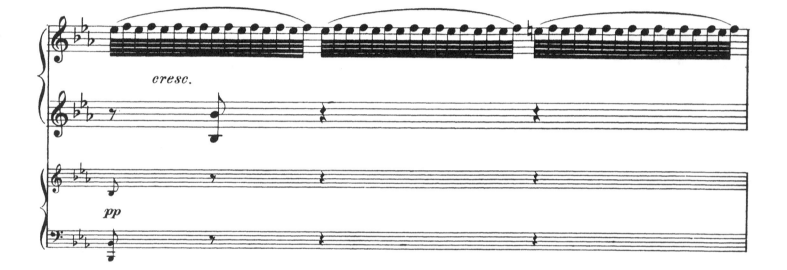

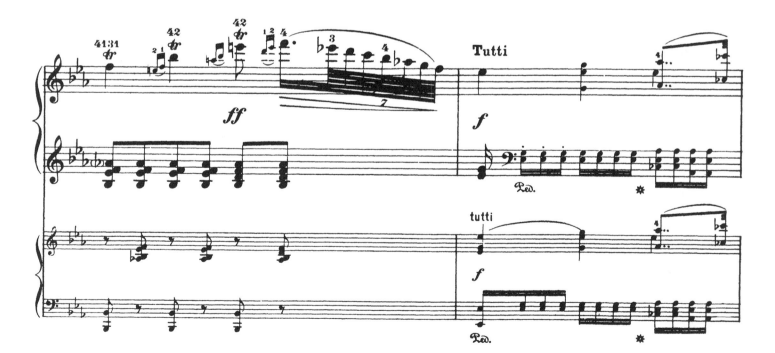

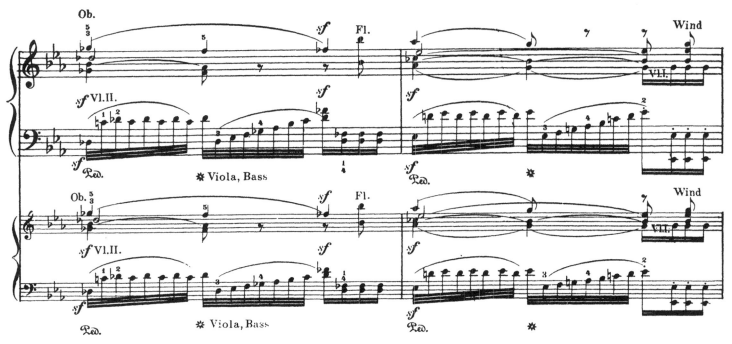

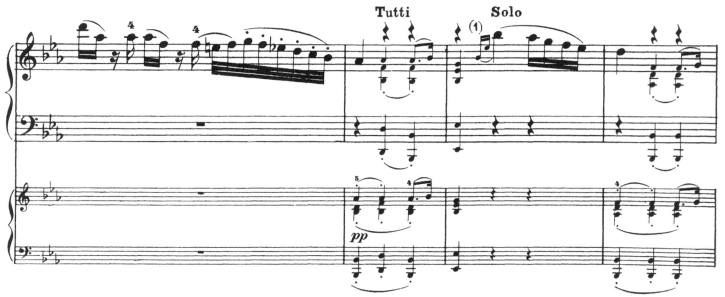

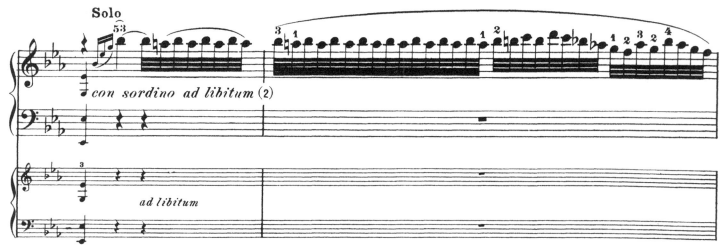

(1) Corrected in Peters, and Br. & H., to ♪♪ The Peters Edition (№ 65) already contains the above simplification of the embellishment, but not the above-mentioned one by Czerny (№ 3695).

(2) Peters (№ 65) writes *"con sordino, ad libitum"*. The insertion of the comma is quite to the point, because the *"ad libitum"* can refer only to the *tempo*, as may be seen from the orchestral direction in the same place.

Rondo.

Allegro molto. (M.M. ♩. = 104; acc. to Czerny, 112.)

(1) Here without expression-mark. At the repeat, *p.* — Except in a few places noted further on (see p. 37), the original Tutti-arrangement of this movement contains no expression-marks except the oft-recurring *sf*.

(2) Staccato, in analogy with the parallel passage on p. 43.

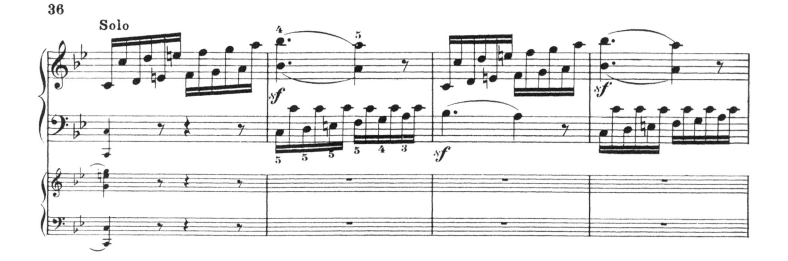

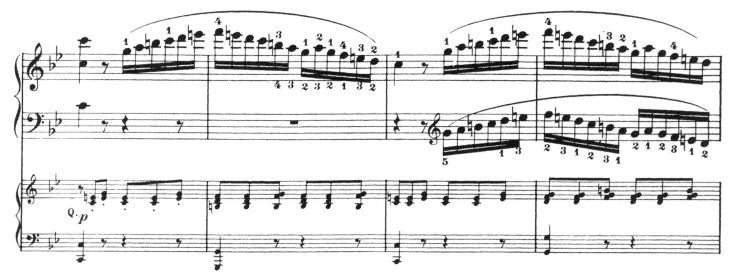

(1) Originally ♩♩♩ . But *cf* the parallel passage on p. 44.

(2) Here, in the old Tutti-arrangement, "*f*"[!], and then, to the closing Tutti, no further expression-marks except the *sf*.

(3) According to the Autograph and the original parts, "*f*," then "*sf*," in the instruments bearing the melody.(The *sf* for the viola is omitted here in the original part; in the parallel passage on p. 45 it is merely inadvertently misplaced.)

(1) In Peters and Br. & H., *"staccato"*. — Peters (№ 65) reads ![music] The staccato-signs also occur in the Czerny-Peters Edition № 3695, though without the additional *"p cresc."*

(2) The two Peters editions just mentioned have, at the beginning of this measure, *"f"*, followed two measures later by *"p"*, then in the next measure by *"cresc."*, etc.

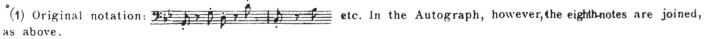

*(1) Original notation: etc. In the Autograph, however, the eighth-notes are joined, as above.

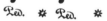

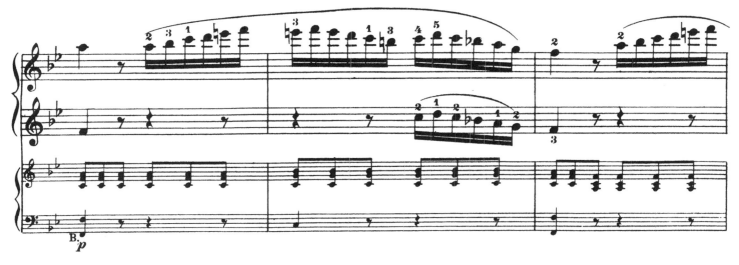

(1) Slurs and dots in analogy with the parallel passage on p. 37.

(2) But *cf.* Note on p. 38.

(3) Violin I has *a*, acc. to the Autograph; the original part, and also the scores of Peters and Breitkopf & Härtel, have, on the contrary, only a ♮ (no doubt by mistake).

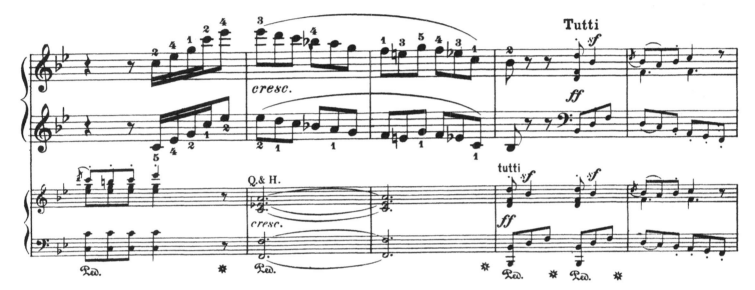

(1) The word "Solo" was originally placed a little further to the right, so that it might seem doubtful whether the *bb* was meant to be included. But this *bb* is already written *large*; besides, just here a bit of piano-sketch in the Autograph begins with this *bb* (in the right hand).

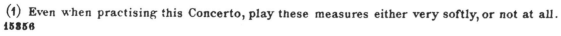

(1) Even when practising this Concerto, play these measures either very softly, or not at all.

(1) The notation agrees with the Autograph and Br. & H.'s score. According to the original viola-part it would read: (evidently wrong). The two preceding measures are simply provided with marks of repetition.

(2) This fingering is also recommended by Czerny.

Appendix.

Cadenza[1]
to the First Movement.

(1) This Cadenza is given, in Nottebohm's Thematic Catalogue of Beethoven's compositions (Second Edition, p. 153), among the authentic works without opus-number; the Autograph, according to an appended note, is in the possession of Breitkopf & Härtel. Not published during the composer's lifetime, it was printed for the first time, so far as we know, by the above firm. We have taken the liberty of providing this interesting piece with expression-marks, which, being engraved in smaller type, will be recognizable as not belonging to the original edition. — For youthful players, this Cadenza hardly appears suitable.

(2) A copy of this Cadenza, from Prof. Fischhof's literary remains (now in the Royal Library, Berlin), reads g♭.

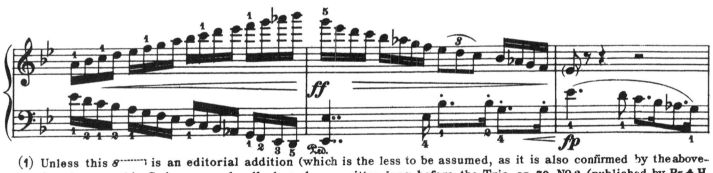

(1) Unless this *8 _ _ _ _* is an editorial addition (which is the less to be assumed, as it is also confirmed by the above-mentioned copy), this Cadenza can hardly have been written long before the Trio op. 70, № 2 (published by Br. & H. in 1809, register 1840), as it was not until about this time that the composer employed e^4b and f^4 in notation (in the G-major Concerto he does not yet reach d^4). Certain peculiarities of style, which remind the editor of op. 101 and 106 (the latter composed about 1818), tend to indicate an even later period of composition than that of the Trio. [Cf. Nottebom, "Neue Beethoveniana XLIII" (in the "Musikalisches Wochenblatt", Vol. X, № 31), according to which the compass of the piano had been extended to f^4 as early as the end of 1808.]

(1) The above-mentioned copy also reads only ♮ (+g).

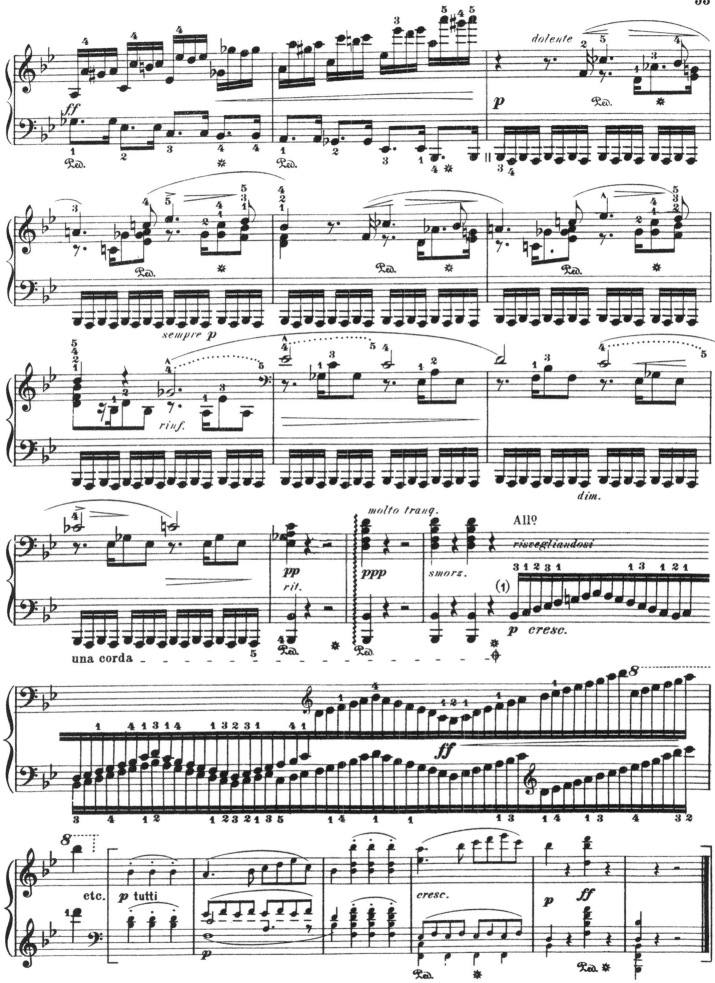

(1) The customary trill is avoided in this closing passage, as at the close of the Rondo of the E♭- major Concerto.